McMaster University

Published in 2007 by
Binea Press, Inc.
512-1673 Richmond Street
London, Ontario, Canada N6G 2N3

Tel: 519.660.6424
Fax: 519.660.4449

E-mail: bineapress@bellnet.ca
www.bineapress.com

Distributed by:

Binea Press Inc.
519.660.6424

Library and Archives Canada Cataloguing in Publication

Bain, Richard (Richard G.), 1954-

McMaster University / Richard Bain

Foreword by Martin Short

ISBN 978-0-9736863-7-1

1. McMaster University - Pictorial works. I. Title.

LE3.M333B35 2007   378.713'52   C2007-901355-4

Copyright @ 2007 by Binea Press, Inc.

Design by Response Generators
London, Ontario, Canada
Tel: 519.432.4932
www.rgdirect.com

Printed in Canada by Friesens Corporation
Altona, Manitoba

McMaster University

RICHARD BAIN

Foreword by
Martin Short

With gratitude and affection, this book is dedicated to:

Chancellor Melvin M. Hawkrigg '52 and Marilyn Hawkrigg Hon '00

You have honoured the McMaster Community with your inspiring commitment, the warmth and grace with which you've carried out your duties and your sincere belief in McMaster, its mission and its people. You are both true McMaster treasures!

Foreword

The day McMaster University started naming buildings after my dead professors was the day I realized that I wasn't necessarily the youngest man in the room. Don't get me wrong – I'm still terribly vital and vigorous and, given the correct lighting and double sided tape on the lens, some will infer I'm timeless (although they're usually in my employ). None of this, however, changes the fact that when I was a student at McMaster, Henry Thode was the University president, not a red-brick library.

Today, there are probably more McMaster alumni who know the library better than they know the man and that makes me just a little bit sad. Like most Mac grads who are not on campus every day, I wonder from time to time if the McMaster University that has been so important to my career and my life exists only in my memory.

The magic of McMaster, however, is that no matter how much it changes, the place you remember is still there. Mac is still the creative, social, inclusive place you recall from your student days. It's just shinier now, with more washrooms. The professors can still amaze you with the things they know and discover, staff can still save your bacon when you need it the most, and the students can still open your eyes and open doors that you will be walking through for the rest of your life.

McMaster University is a special place, and being able to keep just a little reminder of that in this book is real privilege, I must say.

Next time I'm home, I'll meet you at Faculty Hollow for some tray-bogganing.

Martin Short '72

Ivy grows on University Hall, one of the six original buildings built in 1930 when McMaster moved from its original home in Toronto to Hamilton.

As I look back, it was always sunny on campus. The sun was hot across the wide fields which surrounded the neo Gothic buildings and the overgrown meadow to the south. It streamed through the narrow windows in the stacks where I browsed through fascinating books not in my courses. Through the tall windows, it brightened the black gowns required for daily chapel in Convocation Hall.

Inside in the lecture halls, McMaster opened the door to the world of the spirit and the wealth of other cultures as well as the strict academic disciplines. To the child of a restricted B.C. ghetto, there was an exhilarating sense of infinite horizons and possibilities. It was there that I laid down a store of treasures which I have been drawing on all my life into my retirement.

Today the physical campus is a very different place, but I feel the same sense of excitement among the students. I am happy that the University has kept its sense of purpose and connects me to the generations of students who will be as enriched as I was six decades ago.

Margaret Lyons BA '49
D.Litt. '96
Retired VP, English Radio, CBC

Hamilton Hall once served as the Science Building, housed the MSU and many student services and today is home to the James Stewart Centre for Mathematics.

A spring time skate across campus.

Magnolia trees blossom in front of Mills Memorial Library.

ABOVE: MARAUDER RUGBY PLAYER BREAKS FROM THE SCRUM WITH RIVAL TEAM, WESTERN MUSTANGS.

LEFT: CYCLISTS FROM THE MCMASTER VARSITY CYCLING CLUB OUT FOR A PRACTICE SPIN.

Entertaining the crowds at the Air band competition during Welcome Week festivities.

Student life at McMaster is better than ever. Despite the ever-growing student population, the sense of community both on and off campus is incredible and grows stronger each year. McMaster is at the centre of a diverse and inclusive hub that emphasizes each student's way of living while attending McMaster. This unique community makes the day-to-day stresses of student life much easier to overcome, and creates a positive learning environment.

John Popham BA '05
President & CEO, McMaster Students Union, 2006-2007

In pursuit of the Welcome Week Cup, students compete in the IRC Bed Races.

At McMaster we are fortunate to have a multicultural community. This is a community comprised of students and staff who believe in McMaster and who believe in each other. The spirit of McMaster is able to live on throughout generations, this is something that is real, it shows compassion and pride for our school, it shows McMaster has a tradition of producing futures, hopes and dreams.

Jacqueline Cavalheiro
Undergraduate Student, Humanities
Maroons Spirit Leader

Ready to greet the first year students during Welcome Week activities.

New students receive a warm welcome to Hedden Hall Residence and quickly get into the Marauder spirit.

New friends and great memories are made before the start of the academic year.

Distance poses no barrier to my links with McMaster. When our alumni members meet, over golf or beer, we always reminisce about the time we spent at Mac. We relish it when University officials visit us as we get to catch up with the latest developments on campus, while tucking into some hot chilly crabs! We are also spoiled by the very regular electronic DAILeNEWS and the hardcopy McMaster Times. Wow. Mac, you are always on my radar screen.

Patrick Guong-Ching Tan B.Eng. '70, M.Eng. '72, LLD '03
Singapore Alumni Branch Volunteer

ABOVE: ENGINEERING STUDENTS GEAR UP FOR THE
ACADEMIC YEAR WITH A TUNE-UP ON THEIR RED MASCOT.

RIGHT: "THE IRON RING", ERECTED BY THE CLASS OF 2001 WAS LATER MODIFIED BY
THE MECHANICAL ENGINEERING CLASS OF 2005 AS PART OF KIPLING ACTIVITIES.

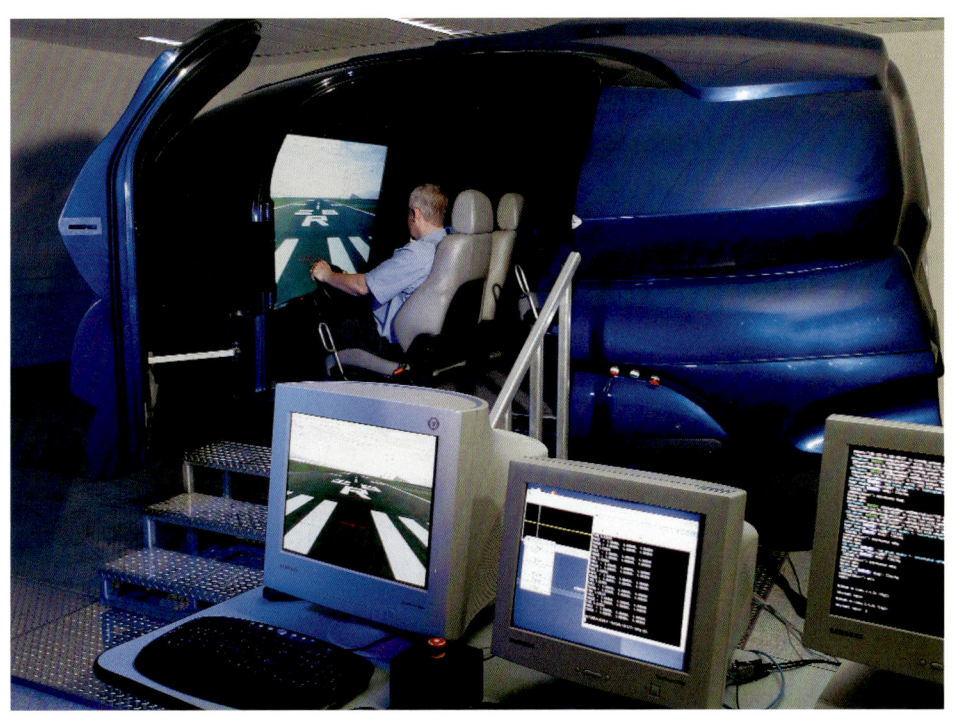

TOP: DR. M. V. MOHRENSCHILDT, CHAIR COMPUTING AND SOFTWARE, IN THE NEW MOTION SIMULATOR TESTING FLIGHT SIMULATION SOFTWARE.

BOTTOM: CENTRE FOR EMERGING DEVICE TECHNOLOGIES-MOLECULAR BEAM EPITAXY LABORATORY. PICTURED ARE RAFAEL KLEIMAN, DIRECTOR OF THE CEDT AND RESEARCH ENGINEERS GRAHAM PEARSON AND JACK WOJCIK.

LEFT: LARGE SCALE STRUCTURAL TESTING AT THE CIVIL ENGINEERING APPLIED DYNAMICS LAB.

The McMaster Nuclear Reactor is the only medium flux nuclear reactor on a university campus in Canada.

It was my very good fortune to have witnessed the extraordinary growth of graduate studies and research at McMaster, both as the first Dean of the Faculty of Graduate Studies and as President. In 1957, the year this Faculty was established, there were 75 graduate students registered in 11 programs. Fifty years later graduate students numbered 2,500 and programs approximately 50. Research, which is an important mission of the University and is closely related to graduate studies, also grew rapidly in the early years to the point that in 1977 McMaster ranked first in many disciplines in research income per full-time faculty member from the Natural Sciences and Engineering Research Council. In 2004, McMaster was named Research University of the Year by Research Infosource Inc. – a truly remarkable achievement.

Arthur Bourns D.Sc. '81
President and Vice-Chancellor, McMaster University 1972-1980

The William J. McCallion Planetarium was the first planetarium in Ontario to offer shows to the public and continues this popular service today.

One of the magnificent windows in
University Hall overlooking the campus.

Looking down from University Hall at students making their way to class amid the autumn colours.

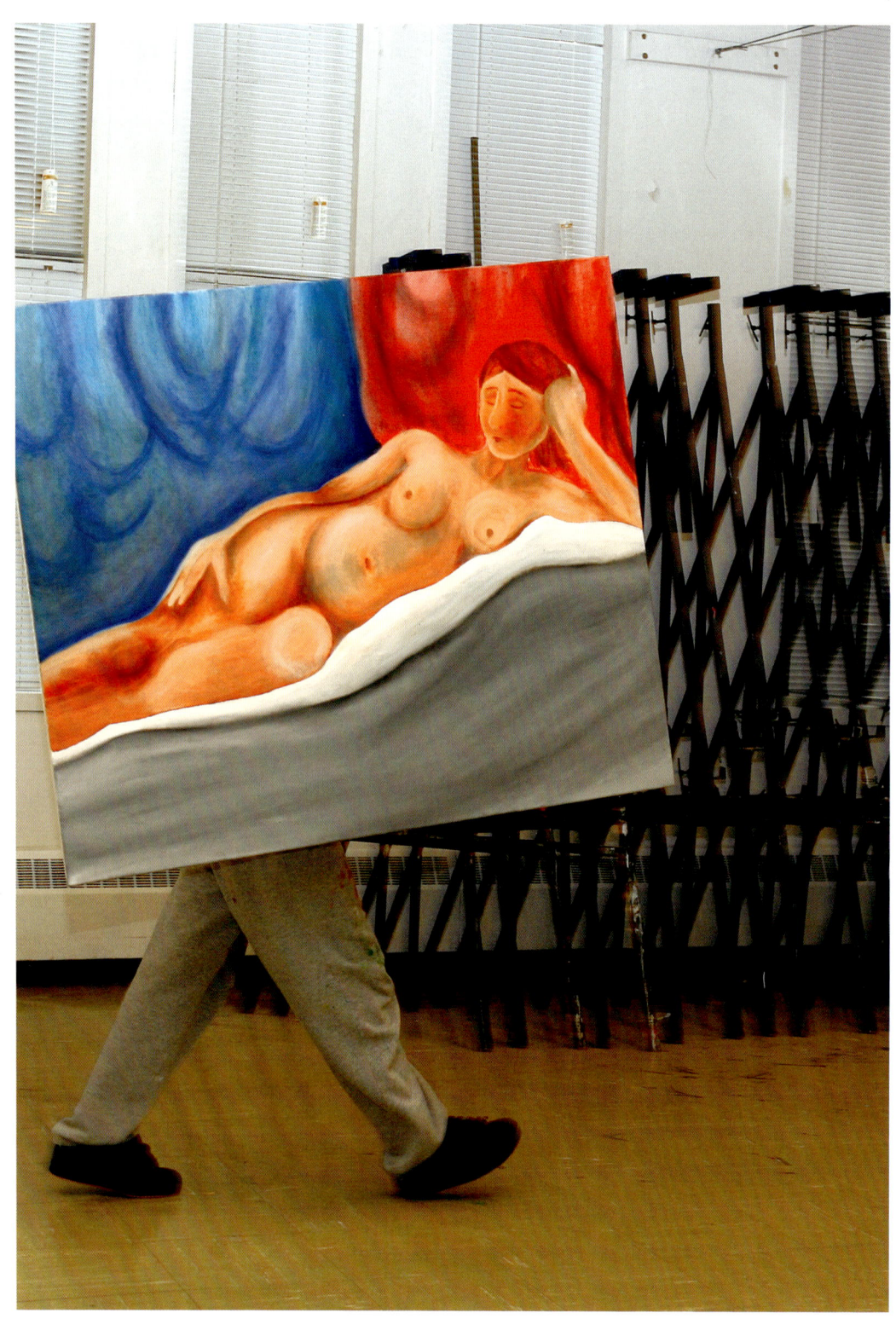

The Studio Art program's personalized approach encourages students to define their own direction.

Students work to create masterpieces in various mediums ranging from paint to printmaking.

The Edward Carey Fox statue in the Arts Quad commemorates Fox's contributions to McMaster as a philanthropic alumnus and McMaster's first Chancellor.

The McMaster Museum of Art houses McMaster University's permanent collection of close to 6,000 works representing the history of art in a diversity of media from ancient times to the present.

Students at work in Togo Salmon Hall.

Alumni reminisce over *Marmors* in the President's Residence on Alumni Weekend.

As a proud graduate of McMaster it is now my time to assist the University in promoting an active and connected alumni association – I look forward to a lifelong association with the school – thank you McMaster and community!

Kathy Chittley-Young '96
President, McMaster Alumni Association 2006/2007

THE PRESIDENT'S RESIDENCE OVERLOOKING COOTES PARADISE
SERVES AS HOME TO THE OFFICE OF ALUMNI ADVANCEMENT.

Convocation Hall echoes the interiors of the great halls of medieval castles, and is a dramatic setting for a School of the Arts concert.

For me, McMaster means credibility for the Hamilton community. McMaster is a world class educational facility located right here in Hamilton. You do not truly appreciate all that McMaster offered you as a student until you actually graduate. It is as the result of my education at McMaster that doors opened for me. Fortunately, those doors were all in Hamilton.

Teresa Cascioli B.Com. '83
Chair & CEO, Lakeport Brewing Income Fund

A FLORAL DISPLAY ALONG MAIN STREET WELCOMES YOU TO MCMASTER.

Officially opened in 1972, the McMaster University Health Sciences Centre serves the Hamilton community as a public hospital and houses the Faculty of Health Sciences.

TOP: PROFESSOR SANDRA WITELSON, ALBERT EINSTEIN/IRVING ZUCKER CHAIR IN NEUROSCIENCE, AND DEBRA L. KIGAR, RESEARCH ASSOCIATE, AT WORK IN THE BRAIN LAB WITHIN THE PSYCHOLOGY BUILDING.

BOTTOM: MCMASTER ANTHROPOLOGY GRADUATE STUDENTS LEARN COMPARATIVE PRIMATE ANATOMY IN THE BIOLOGICAL AND TEACHING ANTHROPOLOGY LAB.

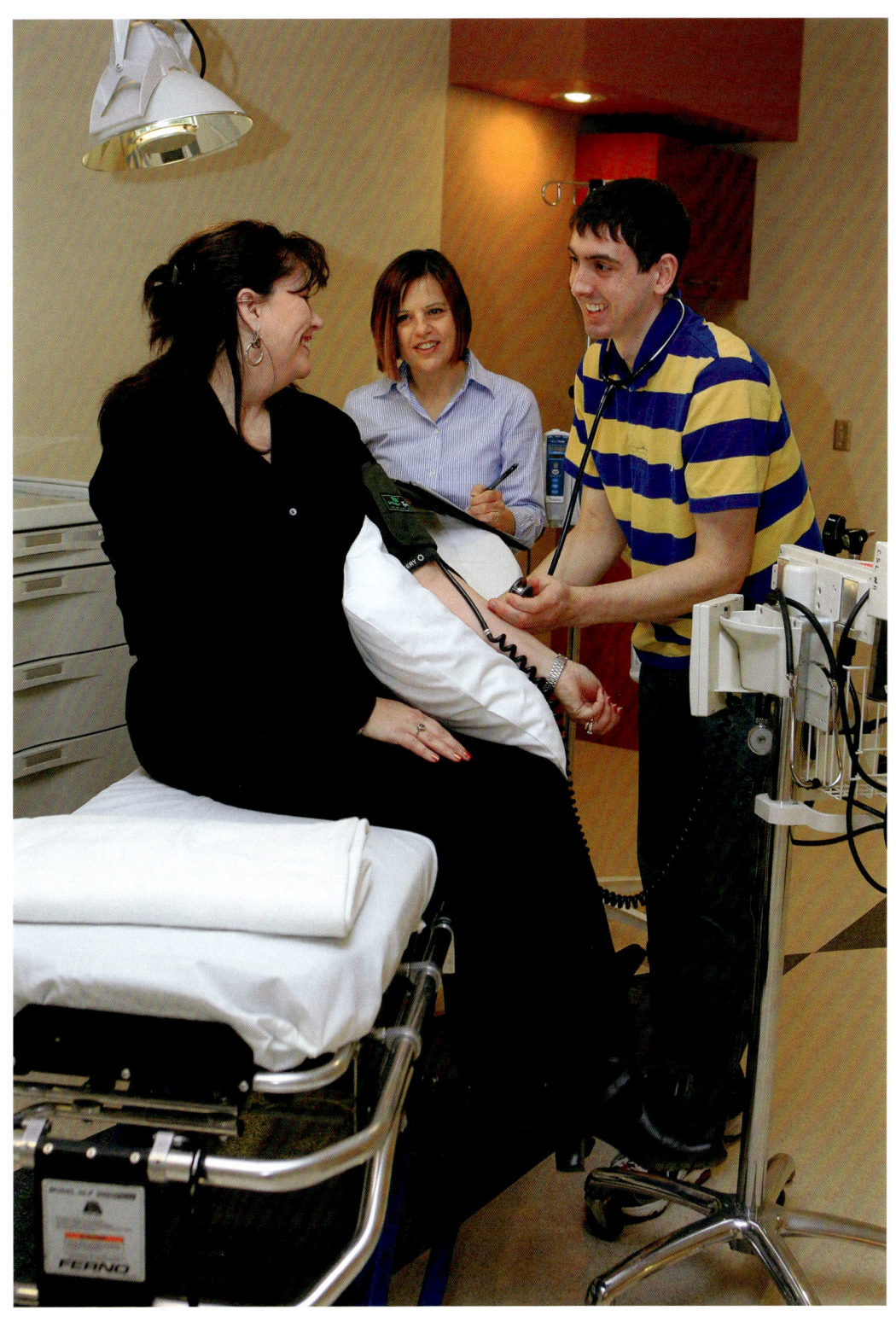

Health Sciences students receive real-life training in the Clinical Learning Centre.

Named in honour of Hamilton businessman and philanthropist, David Braley, the David Braley Athletic Centre opened in 2006 and is one of the largest fitness and recreation centres on a Canadian university campus.

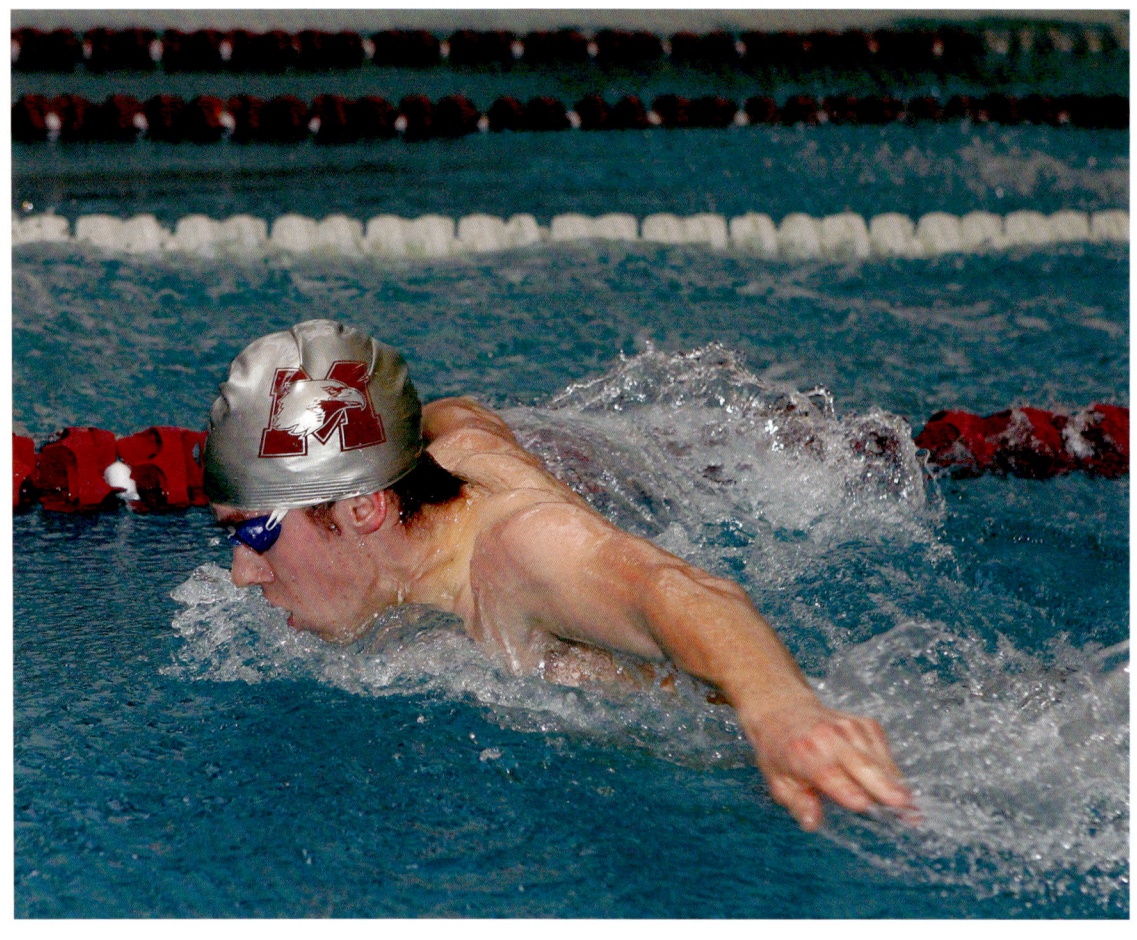

above: A member of the McMaster swim team competes in a swim meet at Ivor Wynne Centre's Olympic size pool.

right: Members of the Marauder Rowing team practice at the historic Leander Boat Club on the Hamilton Harbour.

Anticipating the big game at the MSU-Alumni Tailgate party on Homecoming Weekend. McMaster has celebrated Homecoming since 1937.

The Marauders defeat the Guelph Gryphons at their Homecoming Game.

I have spent the majority of the last six and a half years at McMaster playing football, earning a degree and now working with the Department of Athletics and Recreation. During this time I have been able to build excellent relationships not only within the University but also the Hamilton community that will last a lifetime. I couldn't be happier to call this place home.

Jesse Lumsden BA '07
Marauder Football 2001–2004
Hec Creighton Winner '04

A PEP TALK TO THE TEAM DURING THE GAME.

Nothing ignites the passion of McMaster fans like a closely contested football game.

Maroon and grey became the official colours of McMaster in 1930 and feature prominently at McMaster sporting contests. McMaster's original colours were black and green.

Though its heritage is in the Baptist faith, today, McMaster Divinity College's students and faculty represent more than 35 denominations.

RIGHT: The Prayer Tower in Divinity College offers students a quiet place to reflect.

57

Strolling along the Gwen George Memorial Garden in summertime.

I have always felt a strong loyalty and commitment to the University that has given me so much in life – both personally and professionally. Ruth and I met at McMaster in 1957, when the student body was so small that we got to know almost all of the students on campus. Our University education provided an important stepping stone to our careers in teaching and has enriched our lives in so many ways.

Bob Philip BA '59
Retired Teacher

top: McMaster boasts one of the most
beautiful treed campuses in the country.

bottom: Students in front of the McMaster Museum of Art.

TOP: EDWARDS HALL, LOCATED IN THE HEART OF THE CAMPUS, IS ONE OF MCMASTER'S STATELY RESIDENCES.

BOTTOM: DIVINITY COLLEGE.

Fall colours outside Wallingford Hall (left) and University Hall (right).

62

McMaster's current student body numbers approximately 23,000 full and part-time students, of which, 3,990 live in the 12 residences on campus.

65

The Faculty Hollow serves as a great natural amphitheatre for the Summer Drama Festival on a warm summer's evening.

My four years at McMaster, which unfortunately should only have been three, were four very exciting years in my life. It was at Mac where I honed my craft, my sense of humour, and my taste for cheap wine. For that, and about a dozen other reasons that would not look good in print, I will always have the fondest memories of the class of '70.

Eugene Levy '70, D.Litt. '05
Comedian, Actor, Producer

Campus sparkles in winter's ice and snow.

above: Studying and enjoying the spring warmth outside of Gilmour Hall.

right: Exam time in Burridge Gym in the Ivor Wynne Centre.

A comfortable chair and sunshine in Mills Memorial Library.

TOP: WORKING ON A CARTOGRAPHY PROJECT WITH MATERIALS FROM THE LLOYD REEDS MAP COLLECTION.

BOTTOM: MILLS LEARNING COMMONS IS AN ACTIVE, STUDENT-CENTRED LEARNING LIBRARY THAT INTEGRATES TRADITIONAL RESOURCES AND INFORMATION TECHNOLOGY.

Students meet in the Math Café located in the James Stewart Centre for Mathematics within historic Hamilton Hall.

A MODERN DESIGN TRANSFORMS A STAIRCASE IN THE
INSTITUTE FOR APPLIED HEALTH SCIENCES INTO A PIECE OF ART.

The dramatic three-storey atrium in the Michael G. DeGroote Centre for Learning and Discovery.

The mace, on display at Convocation, symbolizes the authority of the University.

Chancellor Hawkrigg shares a warm congratulations as he confers a degree at Convocation at Hamilton Place.

Celebrating the milestone of graduation with friends and family.

For me, two things come to mind when McMaster is mentioned.

First: as an East End Hamiltonian I wouldn't have had the opportunity to go to university at all had McMaster not relocated from Toronto to Hamilton in 1930. And I'm sure there are hundreds of others who shared my experience.

Second: my admission to McMaster thankfully coincided with the arrival on campus of Second World War veterans, who were either resuming their interrupted university education or embarking on it for the first time. For the most part they showed a war-forged maturity, wisdom, and determination that served as an inspiration for civilian students and faculty members alike. It was a memorable time.

Charles (Chuck) Johnston BA '49
Professor Emeritus, History

DUSK FALLS ON THE MCMASTER UNIVERSITY STUDENT CENTRE – MILLS PLAZA.

The sundial that graces Hamilton Hall
was a gift from the class of 1928.

October colour surrounds Hamilton Hall.

It's hard for me to imagine a richer or more rewarding career than the one I had at McMaster for 32 years. The students I came to know, often at a very personal level, came to McMaster from many different backgrounds and cultures. It has given me great satisfaction to see so many grow, mature and ultimately become very accomplished and successful adults. Through all the years, the abilities, idealism and vitality of students kept me challenged, inspired and young in spirit. What a great privilege it was for me to have played a small part in their lives!

Rudy Heinzl Hon. '97
Dean of Student Affairs 1985-1996
Director, Student Counselling Service 1964-1985

Enjoying the campus in the spring sunshine.

The Nina de Villiers Garden in front of University Hall is a tranquil retreat in the centre of campus.

Getting my undergraduate degree at McMaster was a turning point in my life and certainly provided a great foundation for my career. I didn't start out with a destination of becoming a CFO for one of the country's largest banks, but obtaining my B.Com. degree, the excellent professors I had and the people who influenced me during those years at McMaster all set me on this incredible journey. Oh, and did I mention that my years at McMaster included a lot of fun: hanging out at the Mac pool and at the Downstairs John... people who work with me know that I still insist on fun as an important part of the mix in my life.

Karen Maidment B.Com. '81
Chief Financial & Administrative Officer
Bank of Montreal

LEFT: THROUGH THE EDWARDS ARCH TOWARDS THE ARTS QUAD.

ABOVE: THE DEGROOTE SCHOOL OF BUSINESS.

With its elegant cathedral ceiling and the Moulton stained glass window, the Great Hall within Alumni Memorial Hall is a popular venue for the campus community to dine.

above: A wintry walk by the Michael G. DeGroote Centre for Learning and Discovery.

left: An ice sculptor adds to Frost Week's activities.

After an ice storm along Kings Walk.

A friendly game of table tennis in the David Braley Athletic Centre.

McMaster University Student Centre seminar rooms are great for group work and collaboration.

The Allen H. Gould Trading Floor gives students an edge with real and simulated trading experience.

The restless young minds at Mac are the fuel for innovation, and the inspiration for my teaching. I meet dreamers, I meet change agents and I meet many who are always asking "Why?" – I know I am better because of them all.

Mandeep S. Malik
Director - bizX & Lecturer - Marketing, Business Policy and International Business, DeGroote School of Business

A STATE OF THE ART LECTURE THEATRE IN THE MICHAEL G. DEGROOTE CENTRE FOR LEARNING AND DISCOVERY.

Lunchtime in the McMaster University Student Centre (MUSC).

ABOVE: THE MCMASTER UNIVERSITY STUDENT CENTRE
HAS BECOME THE HEART OF CAMPUS.

LEFT: THE 50-FOOT HIGH ALPINE TOWER IS THE FIRST OUTDOOR
HIGH-CHALLENGE LEADERSHIP COURSE IN CANADA.

I have a long-term relationship with McMaster and with Athletics and the Alumni Association in particular. One thing that keeps me connected is the quality of the people. I get to spend time with fellow alumni, students, staff, professors and everyone, from the President to the guys at the end of the bench on the basketball team, is a quality individual. The people at Mac are incredible. I've been volunteering for over 25 years and know I will stay involved for my entire life.

Don Bridgman BPE '79
McMaster Alumni Association Board of Directors
Financial Advisor, Assante Capital Management Ltd.

ABOVE: PLAYING SQUASH IN ONE OF FOUR INTERNATIONAL COURTS WITHIN THE DAVID BRALEY ATHLETIC CENTRE.

LEFT: MARAUDER WOMENS' BASKETBALL TEAM TAKE ON BROCK.

I never cease to be astounded by McMaster students. For more than 25 years they've inspired me to be a better teacher, a more understanding administrator, and a passionate fan at athletic competitions and student events. Working with students gives you a unique and ever changing perspective and it's a privilege to have had the opportunity to know so many McMaster students.

Philip Wood
AVP, Student Affairs and Dean of Students

LISTENING TO A MATH TUTORIAL IN HAMILTON HALL.

Enjoying a break from class.

The Michael G. DeGroote Centre for Learning and Discovery, houses more than 250 scientists working in collaborative teams to speed the discovery of new medicines and treatments.

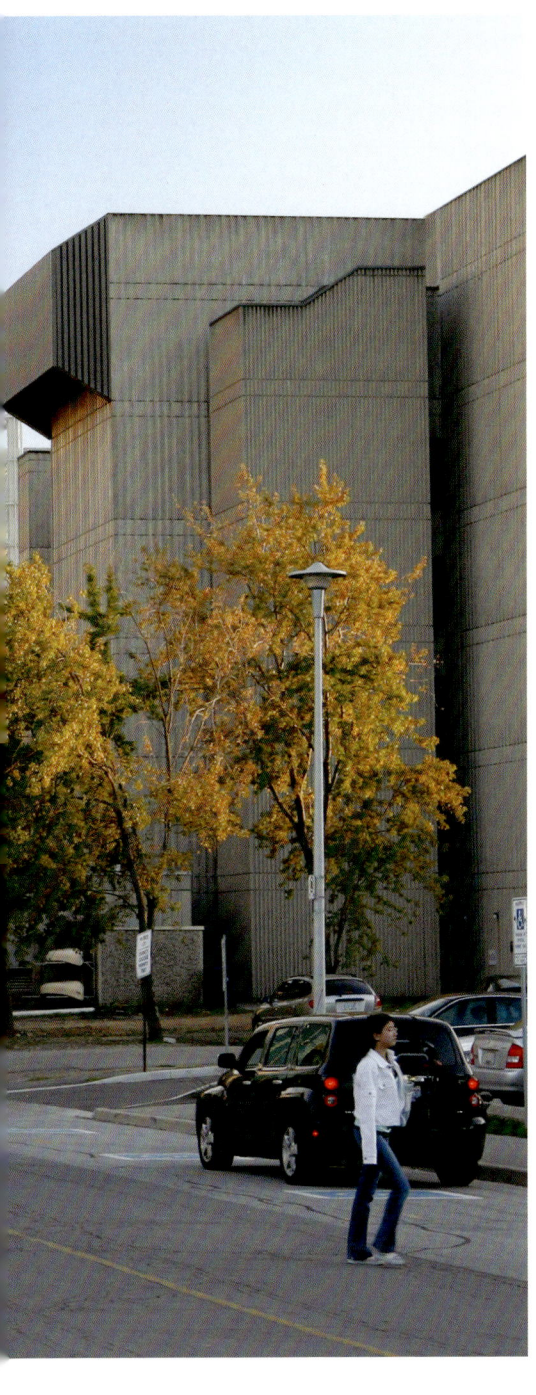

Mills Memorial Library.

LEFT: EVENING PEDESTRIAN TRAFFIC FLOWS THROUGH THE UNIVERSITY HALL ARCH ONTO THE UNIVERSITY MALL.

ABOVE: THE INSTITUTE FOR APPLIED HEALTH SCIENCES.

As leaves fall, another academic year is well underway.

Enlightened leadership is about creating conditions that help people rise beyond the threshold of human achievement. Rather than self-glorification, enlightened leadership concerns itself with cultivating the enormous potential in all of us. As a McMaster student, I found myself surrounded by an innovative, and inspiring culture of achievement driven by enlightened leadership. With a gracious and quietly confident voice, McMaster University's world class academic and athletic accomplishments continue to speak powerfully to our collective and individual human potential.

*Eme Onuoha BA '93
McMaster University Board of Governors
VP Corp. Development,
Canadian Commercial Corp.*

SENATOR WILLIAM MCMASTER HAS THE DISTINCTION OF BEING THE UNIVERSITY'S SINGLE FOUNDING BENEFACTOR. HIS BUST IS DISPLAYED IN UNIVERSITY HALL.

ABOVE: UNIVERSITY HALL'S TOWER WAS DESIGNED TO RESEMBLE OXFORD'S FOUNDERS TOWER.

RIGHT: HEADING HOME THROUGH THE EDWARDS ARCH AT THE END OF THE DAY.

Acknowledgements

I had only heard about McMaster University, until my arrival on campus for a meeting with the Alumni Advancement team, to discuss the photography and publication of this book. I was overwhelmed; not only with our meeting place, the President's Residence, but also with the enthusiasm and hospitality of those I met. After starting the actual photographic work on campus, I realized that helpfulness and genuine warmth was a trait that embodied every person with whom I had contact with. The common thread that embodies McMaster is the spirit and kindness of the students, staff and faculty.

It was an honour to have Martin Short, an alumnus who still holds onto his fond McMaster memories, agree to write the foreword for this book. Today, as he entertains the world with his incredible talent, McMaster has yet another reason to be proud.

Invaluable to this project was the advice and guidance that I received from Anne-Marie Middel and Karen McQuigge in the Office of Alumni Advancement, as well as Roger Trull, Vice President of University Advancement and Dr. Peter George, President & Vice-Chancellor. Many others on campus, too numerous to mention, played a significant role in the facilitation of photography, and I am grateful for their generous assistance.

A group of individuals contributed reflective quotes for this book. Thanks to each of you for sharing your vision and memories of McMaster.

I am always amazed at how a designer can work with photographic images and text, and produce a finished work. This would not have been possible without the incredible talent of Amanda Jean Francis, Brian Ripley and Peter Watson from Response Generators in London, Ontario. Thanks also to Tom Klassen from Friesens Book Division for co-ordinating the production and printing of this book.

I extend my heartfelt thanks to my wife, Joan, who continually encourages me to do what I am passionate about. Whenever I return from assignment, she is eager to see the images I have captured, and hear the stories associated with each one. Thanks also to our children, Caroline, Daniel, Brett and Jordan, who are always interested in my photographic projects, and with my wife, accompany me when their busy schedules permit.

I hope that this book keeps the memory alive for those of you who are fortunate enough to have an affiliation with this great University. I am envious of those who have had the opportunity to spend more than the 10 months I did around this truly beautiful campus. This is a University filled with history, academic excellence, spirit and beauty. I hope all who take the time to visit this campus once more, through these images and writings, remember how fortunate we all are for the gifts that McMaster continues to give to the community and the world.

Richard Bain